Making It Mine

Stories of Teens Who Found Themselves
in Their Parents' Cancer

ISBN: 1979206554
ISBN-13: 9781979206556

To every teen, young or old, who has been
touched by a parent's cancer.

This book is for us.

Table of Contents

Introduction

I wish I could start this introduction with a striking paragraph that is deeply meaningful to you, the reader. I want it to be exceedingly relevant to your life, and your struggles. So relevant, that you wouldn't dare speed-read, or drift off in a momentary daydream because you know that any distraction would cause you to miss a life-changing realization. I desperately want my introduction to accomplish this goal.

But honestly, that's unlikely. To capture the reader entirely is not something the writer has control of. There is one very straightforward reason for this:

Readers, not authors, give books meaning.

However wonderful my introduction, what you do with the pages that follow is utterly up to you. The reader chooses whether or not to commit to the information offered in the book. The introduction does not control the reader, nor do I want it to.

This book uses a very straightforward method to communicate ideas, thoughts, and stories. It is a method something you all, my readers, may already be familiar with.

These concepts are ones that I learned in my high school English class. I was taught that a well-written work must be mindful of the **who**, **what,** and **why** if it is going to be coherent and meaningful to the reader.

Who is this book for, and what is it about?

This book is for you if you are:
A teen whose parent, or parents, have been diagnosed with cancer.

Though your parents may have given this book to you and are insistent that you read it cover to cover, I can promise that's not why I wrote this book. Reading this book is not the most critical thing for you at this very moment. While you are being pushed and pulled in every direction, I'm promising you that I won't do that. Right now, I just want to be the person that meets you wherever you are.

Why did I decide to write this book?

There's a couple of explanations for this.

I was a teen whose parents had cancer. Writing this book has been one of the most meaningful experiences to me. It has given me a way to help myself and to help others. It has taught me that my journey is important, even after cancer. I learned that by focusing on myself I will be better at helping others. In many ways, **I wrote this book for me.**

But enough about me. I'd like to introduce you to some of my friends.

They are a large part of why this book happened. Their stories are real and honest. Each one of them has something beautiful to give. I could not begin to thank them enough for how they have touched me by simply being who they are. I think that when you meet them, you'll see what I mean. ***This book is for them.***

I also wrote this book to give teens something I didn't have. I want those reading it to know there are people like them, who thought the same thoughts, and wondered if they'd ever be 'OK' again. I believe that teens should have something like this book when a parent has cancer. Though you are not the affected one with cancer, your story should be told. I want you to find that story.

This book is for you.

In the pages that follow you'll meet new people, encounter blank spaces to write, read stories, and discover a range of color and quotes. Your participation is completely optional.

When everything else in your life is being rescheduled, treated, and changed, there's one thing you have left:

The choice to live your life how you want, in the best way you can. Before, during and after cancer.

I'm really excited you're here. ***So let's start making it yours.***

The story you tell yourself

is the story you live by.

Part I

The Teens

These first five interviews are from teens whose parents were undergoing cancer treatment at the time they shared their stories. You'll find the layout a similar format in each story: question, answer, question, answer. These teens shared their stories for one reason: with every question and answer, they wanted to tell you that you're not alone.

What unites these teens is the cancer in their lives, yet each story is filled with different insights and realizations. Pages have been added for you to reflect on your experience with cancer, because your story is a huge part of this book. In fact, it's the only reason for this book. If you find meaning, a sense of comfort, even accept a small part of who you are then this book has managed to fulfill its purpose.

Many of the stories you'll read here are from those who have found themselves in their parents' cancer. My hope is that when you've finished this book, you'll be surprised with what you find at the end.

Meet Dakota.

~ 1 ~

Dakota's Story

~ Thirteen years old ~

If you could be any age, what age would you be?

I would want to be eight or ten, because in school
you don't have to worry about a lot, like schoolwork.
When I was eight or ten, life was just great. You
really had no worries in the world. Your parents
were lovey; you had good friends and no drama.

**How old were you when you found out
about your parent's cancer?**

I was thirteen when I found out and I'm thirteen now.

What kind of cancer does your parent have?

My mom has breast cancer.

How did you feel when you found out?

In that moment, I was surprised. I didn't want to show
her I was surprised; I kind of shut it out. I acted calm
and acted normal. I knew if I showed emotion she would
worry about me. I didn't want to show her I was sad
because *I didn't want to put that weight on her.*

I was in my living room and had just come home from
school. My mind was somewhere else because I was cleaning
up. I was laughing about something, and she told me right
then and there. I just kind of blocked it out. She told me
she went to the doctor a couple of days before and that
they had found cancer cells and where they found them.

I wanted to ask her so many questions about it.
But really the only the thing I said was,
"So when are you going for treatment?"

What scared you most?

I tried not to worry about the possibility that she wouldn't survive. My grandma survived, but her cancer came back. My parents are separated. I thought if she wouldn't be with me, then I would be with my dad. It would be different to live with my dad. I thought about how it would feel if that happened.

"I didn't want to put that weight on her."

What confused you most about your parent's cancer?

Sometimes I wondered why my mom had to get cancer. "Why? How?" Was there something she could've done differently so she wouldn't be in this place? I wondered how I could support her, what I could do. What exactly are the cancer cells, how do we treat it and why? That confused me. Coming here, to teen night at Saint Agnes has cleared up a lot of that confusion for me. They took us on a tour to where she had radiation and explained what the radiation does and explained what cancer cells are. Learning more about it has helped me. My mom explains everything to me.

Your questions might sound similar to Dakota's and hopefully you're getting answers to them, either in this book or elsewhere. It has comforted teens to know that only 5-10 percent of cancers come from genes inherited by a parent.

Your questions might sound similar to
Dakota's and hopefully you're getting answers
to them, either in this book or elsewhere.
It has comforted teens to know that

Only 5-10 percent of cancers come from genes inherited by a parent.

-American Cancer Society

Did things change after your parent was diagnosed?

I started to see her getting tired and not able to do more things. I wouldn't go out so I could help her with things. My dad's mom had cancer at the time, so he didn't know how to deal with my mom having cancer too.

Did people treat you differently?

My friends don't really know about my mom's cancer. Only my best friend. She's the only person I wanted to share it with. I don't like telling my friends bad news, like when their attention is all on me. I don't want pity from them like, "Oh, that's so sad your mom has cancer." I don't want them coming to me asking a bunch of questions and me having to explain it to them and getting all emotional. Like that's just too much. So I just told my best friend.

"I told her I didn't want her to ask me a lot of questions and feel like she had to feel sorry."

I told my best friend kind of late because I didn't know how to tell her. She and my mom have a good relationship too and she comes over my house a lot. Me and my mom were done talking about it, and she had finished radiation. Once I told my best friend she was surprised I didn't tell her at first. *I told her I didn't want her to ask me a lot of questions and feel like she had to feel sorry*. Or to feel those emotions 'cause she's really close with my mom too. I told her, "I didn't want you to feel bad because my mom had cancer, and you feel like that's your mom. And I didn't want you to be sad too."

It's pretty clear from the research that there is not a 'right' or 'better' way in deciding how many friends you tell. Dakota decided to tell only her best friend about her mom's cancer. Teens are most likely to talk to friends because they are able to help you adjust to the many changes going on, regardless of how many you decide to tell. (Lindqvist et al. 2007; Huang et al. 2014).

How have you changed?

I feel like I've gotten stronger since I found out about my mom's cancer. I feel like I can talk about it more without feeling like I have to hide something or shut everything out. I can talk about it more freely and clearly and openly.

What advice would you give other teens?

Just talk to somebody. Don't be afraid and shut everything out. Your first reaction is going to be to feel surprised and to wonder why. But talk to someone; don't shut it out. Make sure you have that one friend you can tell, and they're going to support you. Be supportive of your parent as they're supportive of you in every aspect of your life. Be there like they have been for you. Just be a little selfless. Take their feelings into consideration and stay positive.

What have you learned since then?

There's been tragedy, but not something as close as my mom getting cancer. I learned that when something bad happens I shut it out and don't want to realize it. But it's also a good experience because now I know that I can't do that. And I know I'm like that, and I know I can change that.

What was the most helpful thing your parent did for you?

The most helpful thing my mom has done for me is taking care of me. Supporting me like she usually does. Taking me to my friend's house, taking me to the mall, stuff like that. Doing a lot of extra work for me. I'm beginning to make my own decisions and she respects that I want to do stuff by myself, go to the mall, go to my friend's house, go to parties and stuff. Even undergoing cancer, she still allows me to do that, and she's still supportive.

Did your siblings react differently than you?

I don't know what my older brother's reaction is like. He's twenty. By the time we moved, he had already been in college. I think my mom told him on the phone, and I think his reaction would be shock. He knows what to do, though, because he's helped my grandma through cancer, so he knows how it goes.

What helped you the most?

Going to church helped me. Reassurance that everything will be all right. Everything does turn around. So I have that hope; I really have that hope that if my grandma could survive, then my mom could survive. My mom has been through a lot of things in her life, and I know if she can go through some of the stuff that she's been through, then she can go through this.

Making It Mine

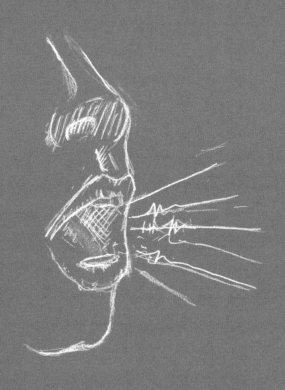

Today, my aunt began a sign language class at a community college nearby. She was diagnosed with cancer about a month ago, and after her surgery, she will lose her ability to speak.

Me, my mother, father, uncle, her two children, husband, brother, and nine close friends are also enrolled, so we can learn to communicate with her after she loses her ability to speak.

-Author Unknown

Blank pages are included at the end of certain chapters
for you to record your own thoughts, draw pictures, make notes,
or jot down any information you'd like.

They are yours to keep the story going.

This is one of them.
So let's start at the beginning.

~ 2 ~

Jacob's Story

~ Sixteen years old ~

What's the best and worst thing about being a teen?

Well, the worst is school and the struggles that come
with school and stress. The best thing is figuring yourself
out, figuring out what you want to do. You get a little
more freedom. ***You get to spread your wings, fly.***

**If you could be best friends with anyone
in the world, who would it be?**

If I could be best friends with anyone in the world, I would
probably say Ben Franklin. I think that'd be so cool.

**How old were you when you found out
about your parent's cancer?**

I was fifteen when I found out my mom
had cancer. I'm sixteen now.

What kind of cancer does your parent have?

My mom has breast cancer.

**What was it like when you found out?
Can you describe where you were, what
you saw, and what you heard?**

She had known a few days before, maybe a week before.
I knew that something was wrong health-wise. I knew
she had gotten a bad call, and she wasn't telling me, and
I was worried. I wasn't talking to her 'cause I wanted
to know what was wrong and she wasn't telling me.

She eventually just caved in and said she didn't want me to
not talk to her. She came down to my room, and I was lying

in bed on my phone. She was crying, and she asked me if I really wanted to know. I said yes. And at first I thought she was going to tell me she was diabetic or something. Cancer was definitely not an option for what she could say. Breast cancer was the last thing that I expected her to say, and that's what she told me she had. So that was a shock even more.

"You get to spread your wings, fly."

Would you have changed anything about the way you found out?

I think she should have sat the whole family down and told us all together. A few people had known before that, and then she told me, and it sort of went through the grapevine.

Did your siblings react differently than you did?

She told my sister. My sister didn't take it good at all. I told my little brother. He wasn't sad; he wasn't happy, of course. I don't think he knew how to process it because he didn't know the severity. I knew he had heard of cancer before but I don't think he knew how bad it was or how bad it could get. He just took it all in, took it day by day. I would talk to my siblings, but I was quieter and kept to myself. I didn't want to get their hopes up that everything would be OK because I didn't even know if it would be OK.

" There's one sad truth in life I've found

While journeying east and west –

The only folks we really wound

Are those we love the best.

We flatter those we scarcely know,

We please the fleeting guest,

And deal full many a thoughtless blow

To those who love us best. "

– Ella Wheeler Wilcox

From what Jacob is saying, you might be able to sense something. Underneath the confusion, missed communication and hurt feelings there is something deeper. What you're seeing is an incredible exchange of love. Between Jacob and his mom, Jacob and his sister, Jacob and his brother.

The exchange you witness between them is tense because of one thing only: He cares about them more than he cares for anyone else.

Parents tell teens about their cancer in all different ways. Just remember, they're new to this too.

What scared you most about your parent's cancer?

I was thinking her cancer was going to get really bad, and she wasn't going to end up living. I just thought that was the end. I was most scared that her cancer would move and travel to another part of her body and end up being worse than what it was in the first place and take her.

"It was helpful to hear her story."

What confused you about your parent's cancer?

My mom didn't really explain what cancer was to me. I don't even think she knew. I wasn't really even focused on that; I was just trying to take it all in. I would eventually find out and get information, but I didn't right then and there.

I already knew cancer was deadly. I researched it on the Internet a little bit and talked to my friends. My one friend's mother had it, and she had a full mastectomy. She started telling me what to expect and the process and stuff. *It was helpful to hear her story.*

Did things change after your parent was diagnosed?

My attitude changed after my mom was diagnosed. I wouldn't say that my attitude got bad toward her, I just sort of had a bad attitude with everything. 'Cause I just felt like everything was falling apart, and I had a bad outlook on life. *I felt my life and my family were falling apart.* My stress levels changed. After that is when I really started to put on weight, probably from stress-eating because that was my way to cope with stuff. To eat.

"I felt my life and my family were falling apart."

Did your friends treat you differently?

My friends treated me with more sympathy. That's when I started to feel hopeless. I had everyone coming to me, which made me feel like my mom's cancer was going to go further, because everyone was coming. I don't think they could have done anything differently. They were worried because my friends like my mother.

My attitude was changing so I had a negative outlook on everything. I probably moved away from my friends during my mom's cancer.

" You gain strength, courage, and confidence by every experience in which you really stop to look fear in the face. You must do the thing which you think you cannot do."

- Eleanor Roosevelt

Did your parent lose her hair?

It didn't bother me when my mom lost her hair. She was still alive. I even told her, *"Hair or no hair, I don't care."* But it was definitely an eye opener, a shock.

I had never seen her without hair. It was kind of one those moments that hit you. I got used to it. I've probably gotten used to seeing her without hair. She has a wig that she puts on to show people, but because she works and is always in and out going to her other job she'll put on her hat. She just has a little hat on all the time.

I noticed some people look when we're out. I think that when people look, they know. They can tell what caused it. And then they like, not back off, but they know why she doesn't have hair.

It doesn't bother me because I've always said people can think what they think and do what they do, and it doesn't have to affect you. I've told my mom that. I think she's accepted how she looks.

"Hair or no hair, I don't care."

When she first completely lost her hair it kind of hit her. But then she started getting used to it; she started liking it; I guess it just stuck.

Like Jacob's mom, your parent may have lost his or her hair. If your parent didn't lose their hair, it's almost as if he or she did. Maybe you wish your parent would have. Why?

Research shows that teens feel extremely conflicted by their parents' appearance throughout cancer treatment. A parent losing his or her hair is a physical representation of one's illness. This makes it feel very real.

At the same time, a parent **not** losing his or her hair and appearing healthy has actually shown to be just as stressful, if not more stressful than if your parent were to lose his or her hair. (Lindqvist, et al. 2007, 349).

While seeing your parent healthy would seem reassuring, it's not. Your parent looking healthy on the outside means you expect them to be healthy on the inside– all the while knowing cancer is on the inside.

In both scenarios, know that your parent's appearance is a poor representation of his or her health. Hair loss is simply a side effect of chemotherapy, the treatment used to kill the cancer cells. The lack of hair loss means chemotherapy is not apart of your parent's treatment.

All these feelings are a result of fear. Research by Shapiro and Shapiro (2013) refer to this as:

False evidence appearing real.

FE

False *Evidence*

AR

Appearing   Real

As a family, did you learn anything having faced this together?

We know now that cancer is very serious and you should always take it seriously and never make fun of it. And always show compassion and sympathy for the person that has it because whatever you're going through, they're probably going through it ten times worse. And to just know that they're not as good off as you.

There was never really a person in the family that had cancer, maybe one but none that we were really close with. It's one of those things where you think it'll never happen to you, and when it does it really hits you hard.

People don't know how to deal with it at first, and once they do, [they] cope and deal with it. It becomes normal for them. It became normal for us.

What is normal to you?

Normal is knowing that my mother had hair, and now she doesn't.

Before she didn't have to do chemo and now she does. I'm realizing now that the chemo and radiation are a part of her life, at least right now.

We all kind of realized that and knew she'd be put through a lot. It preyed on my mind a lot at first, but then it sort of went away. So I wouldn't think about it, and then I would get more upset because I wasn't thinking about it. I tried to block it out.

That can be helpful, but I wouldn't block it out all the way because it's always still there. I think it's OK to ignore it sometimes because you have to get used to. But I still think it's important to know that it's always there, for the time being, ***until it's not anymore.***

Looking back, if you could give yourself any piece of advice back then, what would you have said?

I would tell myself to stay positive. Prepare for the worst and hope for the best. It was hard to stay positive in the beginning. It might be easier to stay positive now that I know what's come of it. I wouldn't say it

"...until it's not anymore."

would be smooth sailing, but it's going at its own pace which is good to some degree. It's not rapid and always changing where you can't even keep up with it.

What has helped you?

To know that she doesn't have cancer anymore. She just still has to do chemo. Because they found cancer cells in the lymph nodes, and the lymph nodes are filters for the whole body. They knew the cancer cells could have moved. I know that she still has to do chemo and radiation.

What was the most helpful thing your parent did for you?

The most helpful thing my mom did was just to be there. Everybody was there. I think I became a little more

LOOK CANCER, THE BALDNESS OR THE HAIR, IN THE FACE.

AND DON'T FOR ONE SECOND LET IT HAVE THE FINAL SAY.

independent and kind of did a lot of stuff on my own.

How have you changed since your parent's cancer?

I would say I've changed for the better a little bit. But there will always be a part of me that knows she had cancer and had to go through everything she went through. And she'll still continue going through it for however long.

And to know that there's always a chance the cancer could end up coming back. I deal with that by hoping for the best but preparing for the worst that could happen. Hoping that it's gone and that it doesn't come back. But then you realize there's really nothing you could do about it.

It's one of those things: whatever happens, happens. Because we can't control it.

What advice would you give to a teen whose parent has cancer?

I would say to make sure you know your parent is loved and cared about and always treat them with respect. Because there's nothing saying they could be there the next day or the next week.

I would say to stay positive, to hope and pray for the best.

About a year ago my neighbor
was diagnosed with lung cancer,
and last month she returned
from a week long trip to Walt
Disney World. She called this her
'happy place.'

When she returned, she gave me
a lamp with cherry blossoms on
it that she bought for me on her
trip. She passed away not long
after her trip, and I turn the light
on whenever I feel sad, or when I
miss her. It comforts me to know
that I'll always have a little piece
of her happy place.

– Author Unknown

Zach's Story

~ 3 ~

Zach's Story

~ Fifteen years old ~

How old were you when your parent was diagnosed?

My mom was diagnosed with breast cancer last winter– that was her second diagnosis. I remember exams were coming up. Her first diagnosis [1] was in like fourth grade-ish. I'm fifteen now.

Did anything confuse you about your parent's cancer?

I'm kind of into sciences. So I talked to my biology teacher about cancer cells and all that. The scientific process was confusing, but I kind of sifted through it pretty easily.

Has your relationship with your family changed at all since your parent's cancer?

I don't feel like my relationship with her has changed. I feel like we're the same as always. We've been close for a while. My stepdad gets stressed easily and it comes off easily. I don't know if it's about Mom or about his job.

What scared you the most?

The possibility of the cancer taking over scared me the most. The last time she was diagnosed, she had a pretty good friend, and I think her cancer spread through her neck, and she passed away. I guess that kind of reinvigorated that thought, but I know she's going to do fine.

How has your parent's cancer changed you?

I've set milestones for myself. I'm going to go to college. I'll probably do computer science or maybe even computer engineering.

Did your friends treat you differently after your parent was diagnosed?

I haven't told my friends about my mom's cancer. I told one person at my old elementary. I don't really want the pity. I just want people to treat me like a friend. A pretty good friend of mine, his dad died of pancreatic cancer.

"*I've set milestones for myself.*"

What advice would you give to someone whose parent has cancer?

I'd tell them to do stuff with their parent. Like Mom and I have this show we like to watch when my stepdad is putting my little half brother to bed. We watch *Cheers,* and we laugh. It's all on Netflix, so we're trying to work through that.

What do you do that's helpful?

I ask her how her day is, and I try to talk to her during her chemo days and ask her how it was, did you see any friends there, things like that. So I think that helps. The first time around it was kind of bad, with her getting sick. It wasn't really bad. We could still manage.

You know, I really think I can put
together a great Thanksgiving dinner.

This'll be the second one that I've cooked,
and believe me, the first one was not the
disaster that my family said it was.

Those kids had a pretty good time in that ambulance.

- Rebecca in Cheers

Has your parent done anything that's been helpful for you?

She hasn't really brought it up, [which] has been helpful for me. She touches on it, but usually focuses on her bosom buddies, as she calls it.

So that helps. I feel like I'm doing all right. It crosses my mind, but that kind of pushes me harder, like, "Mom would want me to do this." I feel like this time is for her.

It's always in the back of my mind. But it's a good thing to think about it and reflect on it. She keeps me updated.

We usually talk on the way home from school. She'll say, "Oh, I had chemotherapy today, and I met with this person, and we talked about this." I think that's a good way to bring up conversation about it too.

Like when it's a chemo day, you could say "How was your day?" and "Anything fun happen?" Something like that.

Finding ways to talk with your parent can be tough. You feel like they should approach you, so you wait for them to talk to you. Your parent hopes you'll initiate conversation; but if you don't, then they think you're disinterested. No one wins.

Zach gives great advice about how he talked to his mom in a way that was comfortable for him. Some teens have kept a journal in a central location and used it to talk with their parent when they have a question or something to say. Your parent can respond to your questions in the journal without it needing to be a big deal.

Becoming Real

by Margery Williams in The Velveteen Rabbit

"What is REAL?" asked the Rabbit one day, when they were lying side by side near the nursery fender, before Nana came to tidy the room. "Does it mean having things that buzz inside you and a stick-out handle?"

"Real isn't how you are made," said the Skin Horse. "It's a thing that happens to you. When a child loves you for a long, long time, not just to play with, but REALLY loves you, then you become Real."

"Does it hurt?" asked the Rabbit.

"Sometimes," said the Skin Horse, for he was always truthful. "When you are Real you don't mind being hurt."

"Does it happen all at once, like being wound up," he asked, "or bit by bit?"

"It doesn't happen all at once," said the Skin Horse. "You become. It takes a long time. That's why it doesn't happen often to people who break easily, or have sharp edges, or who have to be carefully kept.

Generally, by the time you are Real, most of your hair has been loved off, and your eyes drop out and you get loose in the joints and very shabby. But these things don't matter at all, because once you are Real you can't be ugly, except to people who don't understand."

~ 4 ~

Justin's Story

~ Fifteen years old ~

If you could be best friends with anyone, who would it be?

President Obama.

What is the best thing about being a teen?

Just living life and not having to pay for anything yet, for the most part. Just doing what you want that's in the vicinity that is positive. I act so I go to the school for theater. I'm on a mock-trial team, a reenactment of things. And school.

What kind of cancer does your parent have?

My mom has breast cancer.

"I just had to take some time to process it."

What was it like when you found out? Can you describe where you were, what you saw, and what you heard?

Five years ago, so I was ten when I found out my mom had cancer. My mom, she sat the whole family down together at our house. She went through how it starts, and then she told us she has breast cancer. My initial reaction: I was really scared for her. Because it was hard. Both my grandmothers had it, and I didn't think it was going to come to her. It's like, you see other people go through these things, and you don't ever think it's going to happen to you or someone you know, and it did. My first reaction was either she wasn't going to live long or she was going to die.

That was over five years ago. I was in shock. I don't recall saying anything then. **I just had to take some time to process it.**

How did things change after you found out about your parent's cancer?

Not that our house is dirty, but we had to make sure we kept everything clean. We didn't want any germs and all of that. I think germs weaken your immune system, so we had to keep everything clean so she wouldn't get really sick.

A lot of people came over; we always got food. A lot of food.

We definitely got closer together.

Did people treat you differently?

If anything, they kept us in mind. They didn't treat us differently in a bad way, more for the better. It wasn't like, "Oh, your mom has cancer, and I'm never coming over again." It was like, *keep this in mind.*

"keep this in mind."

Do you do anything that is helpful for your parent?

Keeping her occupied has been helpful for my mom. Making sure we're around her and being around her more.

Know that deep inside
you are resilient,
brave,

and so much stronger and more powerful than your fears.

-Gail Lynne Goodwin

What has helped you?

I believe in God, and I'm not as religious and "overreligious" as my parents are. But I do believe in talking with God, praying, things like that.

How did you change?

Definitely seeing how my mom has come through has changed me. There are a lot of differences now about her. We had to keep things stress-free, 'cause she gets stressed out easily. The more stress she has, the more likely it could trigger something.

What advice would you give to teens who have a parent with cancer?

Just take it day by day and don't think about the negative side. Or don't think about what you think is going to happen.

If he or she gets it checked early and on time and gets proper care then most likely they're in good hands. Not saying you shouldn't worry, but if that person who's going through it is not stressed out about it or stressing over it, then you shouldn't either.

Your parent's cancer will change things about your life. Justin talks about the change in his daily routine and having to do things differently because of his mom's cancer. This change may be happening in your life, and you'll begin to notice that how you see your parents, and how you see you, is changing.

Change means adjusting and adjusting means seeing things differently. Change is a process, not a singular event. It doesn't usually happen right away, and it takes time to let go of the old way.

You might not be ready to do that quite yet.

Eventually, the steps you take towards change will start to feel lighter than when you started out. It starts with believing that what is inside you has more power than any fear you are facing right now.

~ 5 ~

Jenna's Story

~ Fifteen years old ~

"What day is it?"
asked Pooh.

"It's today"
squeaked Piglet.

"My favorite day"
said Pooh.

- A.A. Milne, from Winnie-the-Pooh

What kind of cancer does your parent have?

My mom has breast cancer.

What was it like when you found out about your parent's cancer? Can you describe where you were, what you saw, and what you heard?

I was twelve when I found out. My mom was diagnosed a couple months ago.

When I found out my mom got cancer, it just hit me. I was like, "Really, dude?" It just impacted me so badly. I was just thinking, "Why? All of this?"

I'm not really one to cry over things. I feel like it's better to put things in the back of my mind. My dad left, so my mom was the only person I always went to. Even though I have a stepdad and I love him, I usually go to my mom.

"I didn't know if my questions were going to be overwhelming or show enough concern."

When my mom told me, she was crying and I asked her what was wrong. When she gets upset, I start to get upset. I started crying. I told her she was lying and wouldn't believe her. I left because I didn't want to get mad and make her more stressed. I went down to my room and FaceTimed my friend and told her I got the worst news ever. "My mom was

diagnosed with breast cancer." My best friend helped me
a lot. Because her mom went through it, so she knew.

I was so thankful that God gave me a best friend that
went through it. She's always there with me.

What confused you about your parent's cancer?

When I found out my mom had breast cancer, I had a lot
of questions. I didn't know how to cope with it or what kind
of questions to ask. ***I didn't know if my questions were
going to be overwhelming or show enough concern.***

If I could rewind back to when I found out, and I don't
like reading, but if this book was out this would be the
one book I would actually read. It shows you're curious
and that you're concerned and trying to take initiative
about what's going on in your parent's life, instead of
just brushing it off like many people would try to do.

Did things change after your parent was diagnosed?

I came with her to the hospital when she had an
infection, and she needed it drained. I've been with her
two or three times. It's hard to miss school, though.

I'm so thankful for my mom. I've come to the
hospital with her a couple times. I always try to
check in. I'm so glad she's in good hands.

What was the hardest thing about
your parent's cancer?

Right now, there still isn't good news. My mom
still has chemo; she still has radiation. And I'm

like, "When is this going to be done?"

The hardest thing about her diagnosis was when she shaved her head. 'Cause it didn't even look like her at first.

The first time I saw her with her head shaved, we were eating dinner, and I was looking at her the whole time, thinking, "That's not my mom; that's not how I've known her my whole life." It changed me, freaked me out honestly. The one person you've known twelve years of your life, all of a sudden it's like they went away. It's scary.

It was like she disappeared. I hate to say that, because she's my mom and I love her.

I feel bad for my mom when we're out. We had a meeting with my principal, and I knew all she was doing was looking at my mom's head. It's not right for people to look at her head the whole time. There are men out there who have bald heads, and they aren't treated any differently. Just because she's a woman, it doesn't mean it's any different.

"It was like she disappeared."

What has helped you?

Being positive. My dad left; then my grandfather and my brother both passed away. Then my cousin and my aunt passed away. That's four people who I loved. When people leave, it's just as bad as dying. I started to lose hope. It was just bad things. I'm not saying bad luck; *it was just bad things*. When I'm mad, I play video games. It takes your anger.

"it was just bad things."

Did your friends treat you differently because of your parent's cancer?

My friends know about my mom. They're very supportive. They ask me how my mom is. They tell me to tell her hi. People I've used to talk to that I've kind of branched off from still ask me about her. It makes me happy to know they're still thinking about my mom. My teachers frequently ask me about my mom. There are people who care, who ask me about my family. There are people who care other than your own family. If I'm sad, I'm not really one to go cry to somebody. I'll be upset, and FaceTime my friend. I talk to my friends because they're understanding.

What scares you most about your parent's cancer?

I just wish that I could tell the future to know worst-case scenario so I could be prepared if I hear something I don't want to hear. Or be prepared to hear that my mom made it through in the best-case scenario.

In my family there are very strong women. I come from a line of very strong women, and I know my mom is going to get through this. I know she can get through anything. She got through a divorce, her family member dying, working two jobs, managing a house. She got through all of that stuff. She's always smiling.

I don't think there's anything on this planet that
more trumpets life than the sunflower.

For me that's because of the reason behind
its name. Not because it looks like the sun but
because it follows the sun.

During the course of the day, the head tracks the
journey of the sun across the sky. Wherever light
is, no matter how weak, these flowers will find it.

And that's such an admirable thing, not just in flowers, but in people– and such a beautiful lesson in life.

– Helen Mirren in Calendar Girls

Like Jenna said, you may want nothing more than to tell the future. To know if things will get better. This is sometimes referred to as the "in between."

Did your parent's cancer affect your relationship with your siblings?

Sometimes I let my brother play video games in my room. I'll talk with my older brother a lot. We're not as close as we could be, or maybe as we should be. We talk and hang out and stuff but we're not always doing everything together. We kind of go our separate ways most of the time.

I kind of explain things to my younger brother. When it happened, I just told him, "Mom has breast cancer." Everybody was like "Don't tell your younger brother. He's going to be so upset." And I knew we couldn't keep it from him. He still has to know, even if they

"I picture us being happy"

think he won't understand. I want to say he understood, but I don't think he fully did. He's only in third grade, and he doesn't learn about that stuff in school.

Things are basically the same. I know that in [the] worst case scenario, if something did happen to my mom, my siblings would be all that we have. There really wouldn't be anyone we can go to that's reliable.

What advice would you give other teens who have a parent with cancer?

I would tell them to stay positive. If you think negative thoughts, those negative things will happen. I stay positive by making myself believe good stuff will happen. Don't be down on yourself. I picture things in my mind. I picture my mom being OK, cancer free and not having to miss work every week for stuff. ***I picture us being happy***; we're not a bad-off or sad family. We're a good family. It's just been a dreary time.

That was a lot.

You're going to meet some other teens in the pages that follow. We are probably different than what you're expecting.

Before we do that, take a couple pages to keep your story going.

Your Story

Part II

The (Older) Teens

The teens you're about to meet are actually not teens at all. They are adults, ranging in age from eighteen to thirty-three. They are older now, but at the time their parents had cancer they were average teenagers, asking the same questions as you and the other teens in this story. Some of those questions have been answered by time. Some questions remain, and always will.

Getting older doesn't necessarily mean having it all figured out. They are still looking for meaning, for purpose, for this to make sense.

They chose to not give up, to keep digging for what had been buried beneath the mess. Along the way they found answers, mixed in with some more questions. But to keep searching, to not give up, they had to admit they didn't have all the answers.

Like you, and me, they are finding themselves in their parents' cancer.

So don't stop searching.

~ 6 ~

Brie's Story

~ Twenty-four years old ~

If you could be best friends with anyone, who would it be?

Honestly, my best friend is pretty cool so not sure I'd pick anyone else.

What kind of cancer did your parent have?

My mom had breast cancer and my dad had prostate cancer.

What was it like when you found out? Can you describe where you were, what you saw, and what you heard?

I was seventeen when I found out about my mom's cancer. When I found out, I started crying and said, "Everyone who has breast cancer dies."

I remember sitting with my sisters in our living room after she told us. They were eleven at the time. I remember wondering if they understood what was happening.

At that point, all I knew about cancer was that most people who had it ended up dying. It wasn't until later I learned that isn't true.

When my dad was diagnosed, I was nineteen and a freshman in college. Because I went away for college, my parents called me and told me over the phone. Initially I confused it with pancreatic cancer, which is a really serious kind of cancer. So it was frightening and confusing at first.

I felt sad I couldn't be with my family but thankful for the friends I had that year. They basically became my family.

How did things change after you found out about your parent's cancer?

Because my mom was diagnosed in my senior year of high school, it was a stressful enough time figuring out college and life after high school. Her diagnosis caused a lot of questions for me about how my life would change moving forward. Also, my mom has more friends than the average

"*people are good*"

human, so the food was abundant in the beginning. I remember my history teacher standing at my front door with all this food, and thinking I barely knew him and how nice it was that he came all this way.

As a teen with a parent who has cancer, I learned that ***people are good***. They don't care if it's awkward or weird that they're bringing you chicken pot pie. People need to feel like they can help, and it's important to let them do that.

Did people treat you differently?

Yes. They continually asked me how my mom and dad were doing, and they still do. I was the type of teen who needed that. Some teens really don't. We all feel supported in different ways, I think.

A Fish Named Nemo

by Brie Bernhardt and Janelle Panico

How do you surprise a mom who's done everything for you?
She makes your bed and cleans your clothes
and finds your missing shoe.
She picks you up and takes you there,
Piano lessons too.
Loves and cares for all her friends she'll never let them down.
Her smile brightens all our lives,
It never wears a frown.

So here I am a fish named Nemo
To help you through your chemo.
When days seem dark I'll be your light;
We'll form the strength to fight.
I know you're feeling all alone and no one understands,
But our Creator cares for us both,
He crafted us with his hands.
So don't give up, I'll be your friend,
We'll look back and say we've won.
In this short season we'll learn and grow,
The battle will be done.

**Did you do anything that was
helpful for your parent?**

My mom was diagnosed during the school year
and was alone during the day after her treatments.
Sometimes my dad was there but not always.

She just had the surgery to have the lump in her
breast removed. I wanted her to have a friend so she
wouldn't feel totally alone during those dark days. My
best friend (mentioned above) and I went to Walmart
that night and bought a goldfish, a fish bowl, fish food,
etc. We put it in her room next to her bed so that
when she was sick, she could look over and feel like
she had a friend. We wrote her a poem to go along.
The fish didn't live very long, but I think just
letting her know I wanted to help even in the
smallest way meant the world to her.

How have you changed?

Lots of ways. My parents are both healthy now and their
cancer changed me and our family in so many ways.

My parents' cancer showed me this other side of life
that I thought was really beautiful. Now I work with
cancer patients and their families as a social worker.

There is something about people with cancer that is different
from the rest of the world. Strangely, I feel most comfortable
around them. They have looked their worst fear in the
face and decided not to look away. At their weakest point
physically, they find strength they never knew they had.
There is something really inspiring about that to me.

**What advice would you give to
teens who have a parent with cancer?**

First of all, I wish I could hug you and tell you I get
it. But I can't do that, so this is what I would say.

It might feel like nothing makes sense right now. This
wasn't how you planned it and it certainly wouldn't
be if you had any say about it. I felt that way too.
It might feel like you haven't been close with your parent
for a while, and their cancer might steal the chance for
you to be close with them again. Maybe you were close at
one time, but things changed. You changed. If you could,
you would treat them better and hug them longer and text
them back even when you're mad. I felt that way too.

"I felt that way too"

It might feel surreal. Like you wake up and for a split-
second you forget your parent has cancer, and it's like things
were before they got diagnosed. Then you remember the
truth, and it really, really hurts. It is a different kind of
pain you probably never felt before. *I felt that way too.*

My advice is probably not much different now than what it
would be then. When I was seventeen I wrote this excerpt in
my journal a couple weeks after my mom was diagnosed.

This is my advice to you.

February 28th, 2010

I don't want to say that bad
things happen to make you
appreciate what you have, and
may be taking for granted. I don't
want to say that, and I won't.

But I kiss my mom every day, and
tell her I love her. And while I
won't say that bad things happen
to good people to make them
appreciate what they have, I am
appreciating more than ever what
I've been given.

~ 7 ~

Ryan's Story

~ Thirty-three years old ~

What kind of cancer did your parent have?

My dad had pancreatic cancer.

Can you tell me a little about your parent's cancer journey?

It started in December of 1998. My dad was having some stomach pains, and it wouldn't go away, so we went to the doctors. He was diagnosed with an ulcer and it continued to get worse over the course of the month. Finally he had to be admitted to the hospital. It was New Year's Eve actually, and my mother called me and my brother down and they broke the news to us. Everything started from there.

" Why, like why is this happening?"

Just a few weeks later, he was in surgery for pancreatic cancer. He was in surgery within a few weeks to see if they could do anything with the tumor, remove part of it, the whole thing. It was unsuccessful; they couldn't really do anything with it. As soon as he could, he started chemo. Chemo was rough; it was really rough. You know as a kid, you hear about cancer, but you don't really have any understanding until someone close to you goes through it.

He never lost his hair or anything like that, but he was extremely sick. My dad was a bigger guy. He was about six feet two, decent build, and quickly started losing weight. He went through chemo through the winter and into the spring. He went through radiation as well. He continued to lose weight and never really had any positive results from his visits back to his oncologist to measure the tumor, the surrounding areas, the margins or anything like that. We never had any positive news. He just continued to go downhill.

We were on vacation in the Outer Banks in the beginning of July. He was bedridden the whole time, getting up a few times. He and my mom had to come home early all the way back to Baltimore. The next week was when he passed. It had been about six, seven months.

What was it like when you found out about your parent's cancer? Can you describe where you were, what you saw, and what you heard?

We were in the hospital room, my brother and I, and they broke the news to us. My dad was as positive as he could be. They told us he was going to fight it, and he was going to beat it.

When you're that age, you kind of think of your dad as invincible, that nothing can happen to him. When I found out, I was just kind of in shock. I didn't know what to say. I wasn't outwardly upset. I wasn't crying or anything like that. I kept wondering, ***"Why, like why is this happening?"*** After a while just going over it in my head over and over, I thought "OK, it's fine. We're going to treat it, he's going to beat it, and everything will be fine."

I guess I was naïve about it because I just assumed everything was going to be OK. Like I said, I didn't know enough about cancer, specifically pancreatic, to know that the odds of survival are slim. So, yeah, it was tough news to take. Still, the whole time through, I kept telling myself, "You know he's going to turn around; he'll be fine. He'll recover." But he didn't.

If not now,

then when?

-Marc Chernoff

It was close to the end when I finally came to grips with it. I just kind of carried on with life normally and it wasn't until the beginning of that summer when I couldn't hide from the fact that the end was coming soon.

How much information did your parent's share with you about your dad's cancer?

I don't remember getting real detailed updates from my mom in regards to, like, "The doctors don't think he's going to survive at this point" or "His chances of survival are slim." I didn't really get a lot of information from my parents. I don't know if they wanted to shield me from it. Or they didn't want to believe it. I'm not sure.

Looking back on it, I think I would've liked some more information. I don't even know if at any point he was given a certain amount of time to live. If he was, I was never told, and I never asked. At the time I wish I did. Or looking back on it, I wish I knew.

I didn't ask because *I don't think I wanted to know*. I wouldn't call it denial, but I kept convincing myself everything was going to be fine. And maybe

"I don't think I wanted to know."

I just didn't want to know. I didn't want that final news that he's not going to make it through the year, or he's only got X amount of months to live. I kept believing he was going to be OK and he'd recover.

Looking back, if you could give yourself any piece of advice in that moment, what would you have said?

I would tell myself no matter how painful or hard it is, to see him in the upcoming months. Enjoy every moment you have with him. The rest of that year, he never got to see me play sports; he was just too sick to do anything. If I could go back, I would say, spend more one-on-one time with him. Talk to him more about life in general. I have young kids, and there are so many times now I've thought to myself, "Man, I wish he was here for me to talk to. I wish I could bounce something off him." I would tell myself to sit down and talk to him. 'Cause I carried my life on like normal. But I wish I could've just had some more one-on-one time and talk more about what it takes to be a good father. Things like that.

All these things that Ryan wishes he would have done with his dad are probably not things you think of doing with your parent at the moment. He didn't either. It's only in looking back that he saw every missed moment– a time he could have sat down and talked to his parent, or just another day to be together.

One of the cruelest things about cancer is that it won't tell you to do any of these things while you have the chance to.

What was helpful for you during your parent's cancer?

It was the little stuff. At the same time as my dad was going through treatment, my mom had surgery to remove fibroid tubers from her uterus. So it was a tough stretch.

We have a normal size-extended family. Everybody's local, for the most part. We had a ton of support from friends and family. My mom is a teacher, so her school did a rotation of meals every day for a few months.

My dad had a lot of friends, so people were always over the house visiting, sending well wishes. There was always somebody there. Doing little things, like I said, cooking a meal or making a phone call or doing something like that. That was always helpful.

Has your parent's cancer impacted your role as a parent now?

Absolutely. My kids are six and four. Both boys. My oldest son loves sports. Pretty much every day he asks me to play something, whether its basketball, or baseball. There are a lot of times at the end of the day, [when] I'm tired, and I don't necessarily want to run around and do something like that. But a lot of times when I feel like that, I'll think to myself, "You know, I could wind up like my dad one day." I don't want to ever take anything for granted and say, "Oh, we'll do it tomorrow." I always think, "You know, let's do what he wants to do." With my younger son, it's the same thing. If he wants to color with me or draw with me or watch a movie. I never take those little things for granted.

Did you have any questions after your parent passed away?

I think when my dad passed away, everyone was ready. He went downhill real quickly at the end. He was in home hospice for about a week, maybe a little longer. Every day was kind of like "this could be the day." That gave me time to prepare myself, and get ready to kind of almost start the grieving process early.

When he passed, it was almost somewhat of a relief. We didn't have to see him in that condition. By the time he was home for good, he was out of it. So it was a little bit of a relief that he wasn't suffering anymore and wasn't in that physical condition.

So, no, I didn't have any questions. I was at peace with it when it happened. It wasn't sudden. Everybody was really able to start grieving. Everyone was prepared. I was able to wrap my mind around the fact that he wasn't going to make it. He wasn't going to be here anymore. So I was able to sit with him and talk. It made it easier for when the time was coming. *I was already living forward a little bit.*

"*I was already living forward a little bit.*"

After your parent passed away, what helped you the most?

We know what chemo does to the body and it was a little bit of a relief. The whole time he was in pain, pretty much the whole process. He wasn't suffering anymore; he was at peace. Also, like I said earlier, the support from friends and family was amazing. I went back to school after that summer, and the support from my classmates was overwhelming. It was special.

"You can kiss your family and friends good-bye and put miles between you, but at the same time you carry them with you in your heart, your mind, your stomach,

because you do
not just live in a
world but
a world
lives in
you."

-Frederick Buechner

How have you changed?

It's cliché to hear people say, "Live everyday like it could be your last." But you know, when you go through something like that, you realize life can be taken away quickly. Or you can get a diagnosis and the end is soon. It's made me appreciate all the small things in life. Whether it's taking a walk with your kids or going to a baseball game. Anything like that. Sometimes I get wrapped up in the day-to-day and have to step back and realize that tomorrow could be final for [me]; you never know what's going to happen. That goes for your friends or family. It's made me really have an appreciation for what I have. It's really made me appreciate all the small things.

What advice would you give to teens who have a parent with cancer?

First thing I would tell them is no matter what, keep an open dialogue. Whether it's with the parent who has cancer, or with your other parent. Like I said I wish I had a little more communication from my parents at the time.

One of the little things I think is important is to make it easier for not only the parent who's sick but [also for the other parent], little things like straightening the house or preparing a meal.

My most important advice is to make sure you keep a balance in both your emotions and your personal life. It can be very difficult at times to keep your parent's physical state and the worry that comes with it off your mind, but it's important to still live your life as normal as you can. Whether it's sports, school activities, hanging out with friends. It's important to still be yourself. Your parent would want you to live your life as normally as possible.

What advice would you give to a teen whose parent may pass away from cancer?

I would tell them the same thing: enjoy every moment. That's all you can do. Even if it's just for a little bit, take some time to talk. Because you know, if you grow up and have a family, there are going to be times when you need advice or just want to talk, you might not have that opportunity. I would tell them to enjoy every second they have. 'Cause you'll regret it one day for sure.

Ryan's story might make you feel like you haven't been taking his advice to "appreciate the little things, enjoy every moment, and live your life as normally as possible."

This page is for you to write a letter to your parent, to a friend, to yourself, anyone.

Communicate whatever is weighing on your heart and maybe has been for awhile. Share it with that person if you want, or keep it to yourself as a way to let go of whatever it is you've been holding on to.

Write, and release.

Your story (cont)

~ 8 ~

Christi's Story

~ Thirty-one years old ~

How old were you when you parent was diagnosed with cancer and how old are you now?

I was seventeen. I'm currently thirty-one.

What kind of cancer did your parent have?

My mom had colon cancer.

Can you tell me a little about your parent's cancer journey?

So I remember before we knew what was going on, before we knew she had cancer, she had gone to several doctors, and they thought she had ulcers. They thought it was more stomach related because she was having digestive issues.

I remember going to the doctors, being in the waiting room, and thinking, "Oh my gosh, another doctor." Thinking it was nothing. Thinking she was whining about an ulcer. But I was a teenager. I thought my mom was whining about some pain in her stomach.

Then she got really sick. She couldn't keep anything down. Just couldn't get out of bed. She was just really sick. That's when they took her to the emergency room and found out that she had a blockage, and at the time they just knew it was a blockage. Then they thought it was pancreatic cancer. And we had recently lost a friend of the family to pancreatic cancer, so I knew that we didn't want it to be that kind. If there was a kind at all.

But after that they knew it was colon cancer. They went on the next day and removed the tumor, or as much as they could.

After that they started chemo. I don't think they did radiation. But they started chemo on Mondays. I can't remember if it was two times a week or one time a week but it was definitely every week. She would go on Monday, and she'd be sick for the rest of the week. She'd finally start feeling better, and then she'd have to go again. It was not a very good process. But it was making her better, right? That's what mattered.

She did chemo for two months. She did that, and slowly she was recovering quicker. Then it stopped, and she was doing better, and she's been cancer-free for over eleven years.

What was it like when you found out about your parent's cancer? Can you describe where you were, what you saw, and what you heard?

Well, we knew she had a blockage that needed to be removed. I can't remember what kind they thought it was at first, but then they thought it was pancreatic and that's the moment I remember. We were discussing it, and I was with my dad.

We had family from out of town to have dinner, but Mom was going in for surgery. I was staying for a little bit, and then I was going to go see her the night before surgery and just be there with her.

But I remember we were there, and my dad said to me, "Whenever you want to go I'll take you." But he just kept saying it, and I thought, "OK you know something different than what I know." And I finally said, "What do you know that I don't know?" He told me he had talked to her more recently and said that it might be worse than what we thought. And that's when they told me that they thought it might be this other, more aggressive cancer. And so I said, "OK, you can take me now."

DO ALL THE GO
BY ALL THE ME
IN ALL THE WA
IN ALL THE PLA
TO ALL THE PE
AS LONG AS YO

OD *YOU CAN,*
ANS *YOU CAN*
YS *YOU CAN,*
CES *YOU CAN*
OPLE *YOU CAN,*
U *EVER CAN.*

- John Wesley

I don't know. In my seventeen-year-old mind it was one thing if it was just a blockage they were going to remove, and it might be colon cancer. But it was another thing if my mom had something that a friend of the family had just died from. ***That was the moment for me.***

Then the next day they did surgery, and I went to school. And I remember they called and said that she had cancer. I was standing at my locker, and a friend of mine was standing right next to me. And I just started crying. And she started crying with me. It seems kind of silly, but at the time all I needed was a good friend who would cry with me.

Would you have changed anything about the way you found out?

I don't think that kind of news is easily delivered no matter what. To tell a teenager that their parent has cancer, it's not an easy thing to hear no matter how you hear it. So, no, that being said, I wouldn't have changed how I found it. I can't imagine a better way. Is there a good way to tell someone their parent has cancer?

What scared you most about your parent's cancer?

The thought that she might not be there anymore.

What was confusing for you?

I don't know. My family, a lot of them are in the medical profession, so a lot of people were telling me things. I think that was a good thing for me because I had a lot of information, and I [was] not afraid to ask a question if there was something said that [made me think], "Wait a minute now." Like when they said they thought it was this other kind of cancer, I was like, "Wait a minute now. That's what so-and-so just died from. Are you kidding? Is this for real? Are you serious?"

"*That was the moment for me.*"

I think as far as confusing, it wasn't necessarily me being confused. I started out with knowing we were going to the doctor because they thought she had an ulcer. Maybe the doctors could've figured it out a little quicker? That would have been nice. Hearing what was really going on, the step-by-step, the play-by-plays. When you're looking at it from a thirty-year-old's perspective, a teen is still a kid. But as a teen you're smart; you know what things mean. The information out there is geared for younger kids, whereas [with] a teen, you'd be surprised what they can handle. And sometimes more information is better because they can actually try to understand what's going on.

I felt like my family was open with me. I really did. They explained things fully to me.

What did you do that was helpful?

When my mom came home, she was still going to chemo every week. She was on nutrition and had a port in her neck. She had to be on that while she slept, and every morning I had to unhook it and make sure she had breakfast. She was weak, so she wasn't moving around too much. She could just stay around the house. But I had to make sure she had breakfast and orange juice and milk. She needed all of those things in the morning. I lived there, and it was easy for me to do it. My aunt and my grandparents said, "Listen, we're going to be here at night and make sure she has dinner, but in the morning, we want you to make sure she has breakfast."

I think sometimes giving a teen the information and also giving them a way to help means a lot. Because I felt like I could do something for her, instead of feeling helpless.

At the time, it was kind of like I was taking care of kid. But looking back on it, I think it was a good thing because I had a way that I could help her.

But you know, you're a teen. You want to go and do what you want to do. So at the time it was like, "Ugh, I have to be home to do this and that. Make sure Mom gets on the nutrition bag and then take her off in the morning." Looking back on it, though, I wouldn't have had it any other way.

"I'm doing this, I'm annoyed that I'm doing this, and then I feel guilty because I'm annoyed that I'm doing it."

You're a teen, and you want to have your own life. I was kind of annoyed because I had to be there, but then I would be mad at myself for being annoyed. Looking back on it, that's a perfectly natural feeling. Because you are a teen, you want to do what you want to do, and this is holding you back from that. But of course you want to be there for your mom and help take care of her too. It was almost like you felt guilty. ***"I'm doing this, I'm annoyed that I'm doing this, and then I feel guilty because I'm annoyed that I'm doing it."***

I wouldn't have admitted that at the time. Who was I to admit something like that with everything she was going through?

I don't know what the response would've been if I would have admitted that. I think other members of my family would've worked with me. I think they would've said, "You only have to be here Tuesday and Thursday." I think they would've worked it out. But at the time I wasn't going to say anything.

Maybe you're starting to see that Christi was pretty involved in her parent's care, more so than some of the others you've heard from. For Christi, this helped her feel useful and like she was able to do something for her mom.

You might be helping your parent with their treatment like Christi. Or maybe you watch a show together, just the two of you. Or you buy them a rapidly dying goldfish.

Whatever way you've found to help your parent, that is a tangible and incredible thing that keeps them going.

They keep going because they know you're cheering them on. Doing more good than you realize.

What advice would you give to teens about how to be helpful to a parent with cancer?

If the parent has to go to chemo, maybe once a month they offer to take them or pick them up. Something that doesn't make you feel like you're tied into this responsibility every week. But at the same time, maybe you pick your parent up once a month, and maybe you stop for ice cream. That might sound dumb but at least you're doing something to brighten their day.

Clean. I know my mom used to worry about things getting cleaned because she couldn't do it. A lot of things I did along the way I [didn't] know if other people would benefit from. But I remember when she first got home, she needed help getting in and out of the shower, which is a very personal thing, but she needed it.

Did you learn anything about yourselves as a family having faced this together?

As a family, I don't know. My mom knows now especially that she can always depend on me. But my brothers are younger; one was two years younger and one was six years younger. I don't really remember what they did. I wasn't old enough to be there for anybody else, as far as them and how they were coping.

I know the person my mom was married to at the time she isn't married to anymore. So I think she learned that she couldn't depend on him as much as she thought. But I don't know. I think he was having trouble coping on his own with the whole situation.

What did your family do that was helpful for you?

I was always there to take her off the nutrition bag in the morning and make sure she had breakfast. But my family would make sure that she was hooked onto it in the evening. That way if there was something going on in the evening, it wasn't like, "OK, I have to be home at six o'clock." I was able to have a little bit of that high school life.

One other thing to mention, this wasn't something that really helped me but I guess it kind of did. I turned eighteen while my mom was still sick and going to chemo. I remember on my birthday my mom had chemo. And afterward she went out and got a cake and came home. *I'll never forget that.*

"I'll never forget that."

How have you changed?

I feel a whole world away from that. Since then I have moved away. I live in Florida now so I'm a thousand miles from home. I'm completely different. You change so much in your twenties because you really go from a teenage, young mentality to an adult basically. I've grown. I think that was the beginning, learning to take care of someone else and not myself. Not being taken care of.

Did your parent's cancer affect your relationship with them as an adult?

I think my mom learned that I would always be there. At the same time, I learned that I would always be there too. I learned how strong you can be as a person too. And I think that impacted all my relationships.

"*But we still went.*"

What advice would you give to teens who have a parent with cancer?

I think teens can tend to feel like everything revolves around them. This is something you can help someone deal with. Because it's not you that has cancer; it's your parent. Yes, it's going to directly impact you, but help them as much as you can because that's what matters. It's not going to matter in twelve years that you went to the mall one night. It's going to matter that you were there to be there for them. I guess maybe remember to remove yourself from yourself. Because they're going to look to you for some support.

Not only remove yourself from yourself but don't feel bad either if you do need to do something. I remember we went to a dance and we stopped by the hospital to see my mom before we went. ***But we still went.*** Because it was important to us at that time, and I just think that trying to find that balance between what you can do to help and also, not feeling guilty like I talked about earlier. Does that make sense?

You Are Wonderful

- Author Unknown

A famous singer had been contracted to sing, and ticket
sales were booming. In fact, the night of the concert
found the house packed and every ticket sold.

The feeling of anticipation and excitement was in
the air as the house manager took the stage and said,
"Ladies and gentlemen, thank you for your enthusiastic
support. I am afraid that due to illness, the man whom
you've all come to hear will not be performing tonight.
However, we have found a suitable substitute we hope
will provide you with comparable entertainment."

The crowd groaned in disappointment and failed to
hear the announcer mention the stand-in's name. The
environment turned from excitement to frustration. The
stand-in performer gave the performance everything
he had. When he had finished, there was nothing
but an uncomfortable silence. No one applauded.

Suddenly, from the balcony,
a little boy stood up and shouted
"Daddy, I think you are wonderful!"

The crowd broke into thunderous applause.

~ 9 ~

Kara's Story

~ Twenty-three years old ~

How old were you when you found out about your parent's cancer and how old are you now?

I was around nine when I first found out my mom had breast cancer. She had it for a couple years before she went into remission. When it came back, I was late fifteen going on sixteen. I'm twenty-three now.

Can you tell me a little about your parent's cancer journey?

So the first time she got it, my parents didn't really tell me and my sisters too much. They kind of just kept it to themselves. They probably didn't want to scare us. The prognosis was good in the beginning. She went through chemo and radiation and all that. She started feeling better. She lost her hair, got her hair back. She started working again.

She was in remission for a few years, probably about five years, before it came back. When it came back, they were a lot more open with us. I think that's when we started to realize it was more serious than the first time around. It was going to be tougher this time, and they definitely were more open about talking to us. It wasn't just them saying, "We're going to get through this, and everything is going to be fine." More like, "Hey, we need to start preparing for what life could be like."

Lauren, my older sister, was graduating that year. My mom wasn't able to make it to her graduation. That was when hospice was there, so it was kind of like some days were better than others. She was still able to get out of bed for a couple hours a day.

On the Fourth of July, we had a get-together at our house.

After that she was just exhausted every day, and there wasn't really any getting her out of bed after that. There were just a lot of people in the house at all times. There was hospice; there were people saying their final goodbyes; there were tons of family members there for the next two weeks. So that was a big adjustment. Just getting used to figuring out how to process it. At the same time, everyone else is trying to do their best to help you cope with it.

She ended up passing away about three weeks after the Fourth of July. So the month of July was just a lot of people in and out.

How did you feel when you found out the cancer had come back?

We knew things would be different. Because that's when we all really sat down as a family and had to talk about things. Things were going to be different. We're not all going to get to go on our family vacation this year. Maybe a couple of us could go but your mom really can't do things like she used to do. My dad was taking off a lot of time from work because he was her primary caregiver. He was there for a while before hospice came in. I think just seeing how my dad changed during that second round as opposed to the first round, when he was still a big helper, but she depended fully on him now for a lot of things.

It was right around Christmastime, [and we were] sitting in the family room. As soon as they sat us down as a group, we knew. It was rare that we ever went in for a serious conversation like that. That's when it kind of hit us. Nobody really said much. Frankly we were just sick to our stomachs. *We didn't really know how to process that.*

135

My grandma passed away twenty-five
years ago, when I was very little.

Tonight, I was at my grandpa's house
when he caught me looking at a picture
of him and my grandma from their
wedding in 1975. In the picture, they are
surrounded by tons of people, laughing
together, almost as if they don't realize
there is anyone else in the room.

When he caught me looking at
it, he came up to me, hugged
me from behind and said,

"Remember, just because
something doesn't last forever,

doesn't mean it wasn't worth your while."

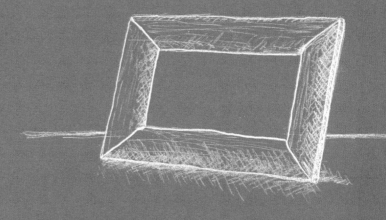

- Author Anonymous

How did things change from the first time you found out?

In fourth grade I didn't really understand it. When you're older you kind of realize how serious it is. When you're in fourth grade, you don't fully understand. You know, like, "OK, mom's sick," but you don't understand what the disease really is and what the treatments really are.

"We didn't really know how to process that."

Then once you get older and you've gone through it once, not personally, but you have a family member who's gone through it and is getting ready to go through it again, realizing how sick the treatments make them. You really start to understand more and sympathize with them. You don't want to go through it yourself, but even worse you don't want to see someone you love go through that kind of pain.

Looking back, what advice would you have given yourself in that moment?

I would have told myself that it's OK; it's OK to talk about it. You're going into high school; you're trying to learn who you are. Then to have that kind of news, you don't want anything that makes your family different. Every family is going through their own silent struggle, but you don't want people to feel sorry for you because your family is going through that. You want to act normal. You want to do the same things as other people. I couldn't always have people over because there were days when she just wasn't feeling well and it wasn't good to have people come over.

Change: the act or instance of making or becoming different.

Did you ever feel embarrassed about your parent's cancer?

I wouldn't say I felt ashamed. I almost felt like sometimes I wouldn't invite people over because toward the end she got really lethargic. I didn't want people to feel awkward and not really know how to react, because we knew how to react as a family.

We just went on. It wasn't always her, and in the last days it wasn't her because of the pain medicine. They kind of lose who they actually are. They're there physically, but they're not there as who they used to be. I didn't have too many people over 'cause I didn't want them to feel uncomfortable and not know how to act.

Did people treat you differently because of your parent's cancer?

I think it's one of those things where your friends have never gone through it either, so they don't even know how to act.

What was helpful for you?

It helped us was when she would say things that didn't really even make sense. And we would laugh about it. She would say funny things she didn't' even realize she was saying. For us it helped to laugh about it even though we knew this isn't good or this isn't how it's supposed to be. But she wasn't in pain. Just mentally she was going.

Chan

Exper

Grow

ge

the act or instance of making or becoming different.

ience

to feel.

to produce by cultivation

Who helped you the most?

The person who helped me the most would be my mom actually. She would talk to us and tell us, "It's OK to grieve, it's OK to be upset, it's OK to be angry that this is happening to you. Just don't grieve your entire life. Don't spend your life upset about it. You can think back, and there are going to be times where you think about it, and you're going to be sad. *But don't let that change who you are, and don't let that be all you think about.*"

Would you have liked more information about your parent's cancer?

Me being me, I would have liked to been kept in the loop more. I would always have questions and things when they came back from doctor's appointments.

"But don't let that change who you are, and don't let that be all you think about."

I'm sure they didn't tell us everything except for what they felt was the right amount to tell us. They kind of told all of us the same amount of information.

My little sister was going into sixth or seventh grade. Sheltering her also sheltered us. I know there's still that line of, "Well how much do you need to tell someone?"

They didn't want us to spend our summer in the house doing nothing but crying by her side. That wasn't going to benefit anybody. That wasn't going to make her better. That wasn't going to make us any better. I think that they were in a tough situation. They did share a fair amount of information with us.

What advice would you give to teens about how to be helpful?

I think it depends on the situation, what point your parent is at. When they're really sick and hospice is in, there's not much you really can do except be by their side and hold their hand. The hospice nurses take care of everything, all the medical stuff. I would say just letting them know that you will be OK. You don't want your parent to think there isn't anything they can do and that they're changing your life for the worse by going through this. Just letting them know that you're strong enough to get through it, and you're there for your siblings and you'll help them through it as well.

Experience: to feel.

As a family, did you learn anything about yourselves having faced this together?

My relationship with my family is stronger now. My little sister didn't have our mom at all, so my older sister and I always tried to be there for her. From first dances, to going to senior nights, academic award ceremonies. We always tried to make it a point, even if we weren't local at the time to get up there for those things. It was a change. But I always knew I wanted to do that because it's not fair to her. We always had someone there with us to go get our hair

Dear Mom,

I wasn't always there for you. I didn't always ask you
how you were doing. I avoided you. I was embarrassed
that you were sick, bald, exhausted. I chose sleepovers
with friends over family nights.

Did I buy you flowers? Did I give you a hug every night
before you went to bed? Was I ever mean? Did I yell?

After talking to so many other teens going through
this experience and spending a year reflecting upon,
thinking about, processing cancer, I can now give you a
window into my teenaged mind.

I wanted to be independent. I didn't want to pitied. I
believed so strongly that you would survive that I avoided fear and rejected grief about the experience. I felt
guilty when I wasn't there for you.
I want to apologize for the way I may have acted, for
the things I didn't do and the words I never spoke. I
want to let you know that I was scared, I did care and I
did want to be there for you.

Thank you for not holding me to higher expectations
(even if you should have!). Thank you for understanding
that I still needed to be a teen. Thank you for forgiving
me if I wasn't always the best daughter. And thank you
for the one silver lining of our cancer experience – the
opportunity for Dad and I to give back and fill a gap in
resources. Now, teens will have a guide to turn to and
hopefully be better sons and daughters to a parent with
cancer than I was!

Love,
Maya

- Maya Silver in 'My Parent Has Cancer and It Really Sucks'

done and to go get our nails done. So she deserves that. She deserves someone to go with her and do those things too. When we were driving to the grave site my dad said, "*It's just me now.* You guys are going to have to learn that it's just us. We're going to make it and we're going to do OK." But in that moment, just realizing, we were down to one parent.

"It's just me now."

If anything my relationship with my dad got stronger. I always had a good relationship with my dad, but when you realize how quickly you can lose a parent, you change. You call them more. You do more things with them because you want to spend as much time with them as you can.

Grow: produce by cultivation.

Kara's story is one of change, experience, and growth. Change through circumstance, experience through openness, and growth through acceptance. Though the cancer was forced into her life, she decided the end result.

She watered, watched, waited.

And she bloomed.

What did you learn about yourself?

I learned to not really hold on to grudges, I don't sweat the small things 'cause in the end it's not worth it. As you grow up, you see how much more you really are like that parent. I do things exactly the same way as my mom. I handle relationships the same way that she handled them with us. Things you don't realize when you're younger, but as you get older and start to mature you realize you are a lot more like that person than you thought you were.

It makes you stronger. I know for me, my younger sister was little so we wanted to be there for her. Even my older sister isn't as good with news like that and with grief. So you learn to be the strong one and to be there for them. Don't put your emotions first and focus on the other person and making sure they're OK. *I kind of put myself last now.*

What helps you now?

Just talking about her. Hearing stories and bringing up those fun memories you had with them. It keeps them alive in spirit. Hearing stories that you hadn't heard before because maybe you were too young to hear them.

"*I kind of put myself last now.*"

What advice would you give to a teen whose parent passed away from cancer?

I would say it's OK to be angry. It's OK to grieve. That's part of the process. That you'll never stop missing them, and it won't necessarily get easier, but you'll be OK in the end. You'll continue making relationships. Your relationships with other people will get stronger. Don't expect anyone to fill that void. It'll be an adjustment, but it'll be OK.

Let go a little and let life happen.
Because sometimes the truths you
can't change, end up changing you

and helping you grow.

- Author Unknown

~ 10 ~

Cydney's Story

~ Eighteen years old ~

What has your experience been like as a public figure, with a parent who has cancer?

I started my reign when I was a senior in high school and I was completely nervous about it. It was my very first pageant, and I honestly didn't know how the whole process was going to work between going on appearances and going to school, because I went to a performing arts school. So I was a full-time dancer, sometimes until eight at night. You would think [for] a teenager that schedule is very crazy, and you're right.

Being Miss District of Columbia's Outstanding Teen in 2014 was an amazing experience. I've met so many amazing people during that journey and so many other amazing people who have also gone through cancer as well. I am a member of two breast cancer organizations and I'm still in contact with them now. They're very supportive of me and my mom and it's also just nice to have connections like that with people who can check up on you. Especially someone of my age, because I get very emotional talking about my mom. But it's nice to know people have gone through the same thing, dealing with cancer.

Through my reign there was a lot going on. I would have to wake up at eight o'clock on Saturday and Sundays and I would be at appearances for sometimes four to six hours. And my mom went to every appearance with me. She was always there. She'd be like, "Cydney, don't be nervous. You got this." She was always there, lifting me up during nerve-wracking experiences that I had never gone through before.

During spring break, I went back and crowned over two hundred little girls, and it was absolutely amazing. It really touched my heart that I got to see all these amazing little girls who had on their little dresses and these beautiful head pieces and their shoes. You could see a bright light in their eyes as six other title holders and I were crowning them. And it's things like that, as a title holder and a public figure, [that] make you feel so wonderful inside. I think that experience was the best part of being a public figure, because I got to make those little girls feel so special. I basically got to be a role model for them, and that's something I never could do before. I love being a public figure. Overall I would say that being a public figure is something that is always going to be there. Even though my reign is over, I know I can always go and give back in any way that I can.

How old were you when your parent was diagnosed with breast cancer and how old are you now?

I was twelve years old when my mom was first diagnosed with breast cancer and I am eighteen years old now.

What was her journey like?

My mom has dealt with breast cancer three times, and it has been a really rough journey for her. I'm glad that I got to be there by her side. Now that I'm in college, I can't be there as much as I was when she was diagnosed each time. I do my best to call her and talk to her everyday, every moment of the day.

When she was first diagnosed it was really, really hard. When I was in high school I was trying to figure out how to juggle all my work. Helping her with her baths, helping her change her drain, and just being there for her.

I know there were plenty of times when she needed me to stay in the room with her because she wanted someone to be there to comfort her and give her a hug. And I was glad

Do more than exist, ——————————————————

Do more than touch,——————————————————

Do more than look,——————————————————

Do more than read,——————————————————

Do more than hear,——————————————————

Do more than listen,——————————————————

Do more than think,——————————————————

Do more than talk,——————————————————

live.

feel.

observe.

absorb.

listen.

understand.

ponder.

say something.

- John H. Rhoades

that I could be there for her in that way. It's been me and her, all of my eighteen years that I've been on this earth. We're like each other's backbone. Whenever she needs me, I'm there. And whenever I need her, she's there.

What was it like when you found out about your parent's cancer?

The first time they told her that it was basically nothing and to check back in six months. But my mom would always do breast self-exams. As a public figure, I was always promoting breast self-exams. Many women don't catch their breast cancer at an early stage; it's usually at the second stage or in many cases the last stage.

"my mom doesn't wear her problems."

But my mom didn't agree with what the doctor was saying because she knew something wasn't right. So she told them to check again, and when they did, they found the breast cancer. They did the first surgery and took out all the cancer, but that time she kept her breast.

The second time, they completely removed the breast. They found another lump on the side, kind of in the same place, but a little above it. They had to take some tissue from her back to do the reconstruction on her breast.

The third time my mom found another lump in the exact same place. So they had to go back in and remove the cancer once again. She just had her final reconstruction last year for her third time having breast cancer. So now she's completely done with everything and in remission.

She's now dealing with a lot of other stuff. She just got diagnosed with another disease, which is attacking all her tissues, called misconnected tissue disorder. She had Grave's disease, dealing with her thyroid and having to get that removed. She has metal plates in her neck and bulging discs in her neck. The misconnected tissue disorder also had to do with all the swelling she was having in her ankles and her legs and recently in her hands and her fingers.

But other than all that, *my mom doesn't wear her problems.* She doesn't wear her pain. That's what makes her such a special woman. Because when people look at her, they don't see the internal problems that are going on with her. She's always walking around with a smile on her face, and she's always giving back regardless of what's going on. And that's what I love about my mom the most. She's amazing.

What was it like in high school as your parent went through breast cancer?

I was in seventh or eighth grade when it started, and then it went all the way up through my high-school years. I don't even know where to begin. In high school, that's when the worst parts of the breast cancer were hitting.

I know I always found myself talking to the guidance counselor in school about what was going on. Because everyone in the school knew my mom. My mom was a mom to all my friends, and she knew all my teachers. They always had good things to say about her. Because my mom was going through a lot, I never wanted to put any stress on her in any type of way.

I had to do everything possible to make sure that my mom had everything she needed while I was in high school. Like if she needed me to pick up her medications, I would go do that. While I was in high school, I would help her mostly with changing her drains after she had her surgery. Just helping her around the house. If she needed me to do her laundry, I would always do that. Especially because it's just the two of us. I didn't want her to do anything. I would cook; I would clean; I would do yard work. So all she had to do was rest.

Sometimes I even put my homework aside because I had no problem with school. In some cases, I put my mom first before school. And when it came time for me being a senior, I had to learn how to put my mom and her cancer on the same level with my school.

I also knew I didn't want to let her down. She always tells me to this day, "Cydney, you make me so proud with how you dealt with me in high school." Because I always came out with straight A's, and I think that's because I had a great support system.

How did you find the balance between being in high school and having a parent with cancer?

When I was a junior, a lot of the work started. I had a lot of stuff done during the beginning of my high-school years so that I wouldn't have that much stuff to do as a senior. Sometimes I didn't even want to ask my mom for help with essays. But of course she was like, "Cydney, that's what I'm here for. If you ever need help with anything, I'm here for you. If you ever need help with anything, you know you can count on me." Even though my mom was going through that, she was always there to help me with whatever I needed in school. So she played a big part in me balancing both.

When did you start to prepare for Miss Outstanding Teen?

It all started senior year. One of my mom's friend's daughters was thinking about doing the preteen part of the Miss America Organization. She was talking to my mom about the teen part of it, and we were both thinking, "It's for a scholarship," and I needed as much scholarship as possible. My mom didn't really have an income, and she couldn't work because she was dealing with cancer basically the whole time I was in high school. We were trying to figure out how I was going to pay for college. When we found out it was a scholarship-based organization, we were like, "OK this is something we need to get on board with.'

My personal trainer also played a very big part in helping us. I would call him or text him and be like, "Mr. Josh, what should I wear this to this appearance? What do I wear to the Cherry Blossom Festival? What do I wear to the Chinese parade?"

It was just things like that, and I was glad that I had people who were there for me and my mom in that way.

How did your role as Miss Outstanding Teen impact the voice you had about breast cancer?

Breast-cancer awareness and breast-health exams were the platform for my initiative. As Miss District of Columbia's Outstanding Teen, I was able to go to appearances all over the DC area and promote my platform in ways that I couldn't promote them without me having a title. *It gave me a different kind of voice and made people listen.* That made me feel even better, because after talking with me about breast-health exams, women left with a new look on how they could approach their doctors and how they were going to deal with their breast cancer.

"It gave me a different kind of voice and made people listen."

My mom didn't have to do chemotherapy. Not only because of the certain breast cancer she had but because she took the initiative to do these breast-health exams all on her own. She knew her body and knew when something didn't feel right. And I have to tell others about that.

What was the most helpful thing your mom did for you during her cancer?

Taking me to all my appearances and helping me with the most outstanding scholarship that I could ever receive in my life that's basically paying for my whole college tuition. That's all thanks to my mom because she helped me with every single essay, and there were eight of them.

The Gates Millennium Scholarship is worth over $1 million dollars. It pays for my college tuition all the way up to my PhD. If I didn't have my mom, I honestly don't know how I would be paying for college at all. Because of my mom, I can say that I am sure of my future now. And it's all thanks to her.

She is really a superwoman in my eyes. When she took me to my dance class that ended at eight o'clock she would have to stay after school just to wait for me. Things like that. In my eyes, it made her the best mother in the world because she didn't have to do that. She could've just dropped me off and said, "Find your own way home" or "Take the train." But she didn't do that. She was always there.

Did your parent's cancer change your relationship with her?

I would say it made us even closer than we ever were before. ***But it was also very hard.*** Sometimes I just wanted time to myself but also knew I had to be there for her, because she didn't really have anyone else. Like I said, it was just us two. Since I was a little girl, it's always been just us. That was the hardest part because sometimes I just would want to sit in my room and have time for myself, but she wanted me to come in there and watch a movie with her, or she wanted me to play Scrabble with her. And I didn't mind, but sometimes I just wanted time to myself. So it was really hard trying to figure out basically what to do and how to balance the two.

"But it was also very hard."

My mom always told me that she wanted me to do things with my friends. She was always telling me, "Cydney, I'm OK, you always take very good care of me, so you don't have to worry about me all the time. You've made it so easy for me at home."

There were many times where I did feel guilty. I would go to her and ask her if she really wanted me to go with my friends. She didn't want me to feel like I didn't have a good childhood because I was always taking care of her.

How do you feel like you've changed since your parent's cancer?

I would say going through this journey with my mom has made me an even stronger woman. Like if I can deal with my mom having breast cancer three different times and even more disease on top of that, I feel like I'm able to go through a whole building engulfed in flames and come out with not one burn on my body. I feel like I'm able to do anything, be put through any challenge and overcome it in the most interesting way.

How did this experience influence who you are now?

It's definitely created more opportunities for me, and it's really helped with being more poised. Me being in a pageant wasn't very difficult because I'm a ballet dancer. A lot of things came natural to me with the way I was raised by my mom. When I entered the pageant world, people were always saying to me, "What? This is your very first pageant?"

"Because I was always there for her, and I always told her that things would be OK."

Starting high school, I was very shy, and this was the only thing that was really difficult for me. Doing the pageant really brought me out of my shell. I'm always eager to talk to someone and make connections. When I was a freshman, my mom would say "Look! There's so-and-so from Channel Nine news." I would run away from that situation and not even want to talk to them. But now I just jump right on it, because I know networking is the most important thing. I am eighteen now so I need as many connections as possible in the career that I want to pursue.

What advice would you give to teens who have a parent with cancer?

I would tell them to be there for their parent in all ways possible, because it's a different connection with a parent. That's why I said it made me and my mom's relationship even stronger. *Because I was always there for her, and I always told her that things would be OK.* There's something about hearing that coming from your child's mouth.

My mom always told me she sees a certain light in me. Like she hears a spirit from heaven talking to her through me. That's what I mean by it's different when you hear your child say, "Everything is going to be OK." So I would tell another teen: Just be there. Tell them things are going to be OK and that whenever they need something you will be there. Because there's nothing like a parent and a child's relationship. It's supposed to be an unbreakable bond.

That's what helped me and my mom's relationship.

Cydney attends Virginia Commonwealth University in Richmond, Virginia. She aspires to be an actress, a singer, and a director and to work in the communications field someday.

She says, "I want to do so many things, its beyond me."

I haven't a clue as to how my story will end.

But that's all right.

When you set out on a journey

and night covers the road,

that's when you discover the stars.

- Nancy Willard

Conclusion

You've read all the stories.

The who: the teens and their parents. The what: the cancer. It's all there. But one thing is missing.

Why?

From the moment your parent was diagnosed, to when you picked up this book, to the now of this very word, you were finding your place in your parent's cancer with every page, every thought, every word you put to paper, maybe not even realizing it at times.

The why of this story is you. It always has been.

The "finding" is why I wrote this book. Why I asked teens and adults to talk about their parents' cancer, even if it was painful for them. Why artists, photographers, authors, public figures, and graphic designers kept saying, "Yeah, I'd love to help for free."

Every why leads back to you. Because without you, this book is irrelevant.

These last few pages are for you to finish this book with your story- the who, the what, the why. Knowing that finding your place in your parent's cancer means something, even if you're still not able to convince yourself of that. Wherever you've found yourself, write it down.

So that one day, when the questions have faded away, you will be left with a clear, resounding belief. A belief that will fill the broken spaces, the gap between what you thought life would be and what it is now. And in that gap, you would find peace, with yourself and with life's every moment. That no matter what cancer had planned when it entered your life, you chose the outcome.

And in that moment you would say, "I made it mine."

Your Story

Your Story

Your Story

Your Story

Your Story

Resources

ONLINE RESOURCES

Grouploog.org — Online support community for teens with family members who have cancer.

Kidshealth.org — They provide materials and information to teens about various cancer treatments and what they can expect.

National Cancer Institute — Resources for teens dealing with a parent who has cancer. They provide resources to help manage stress, to find support, to help teens cope, and more. Information can be found at http://www.cancer.gov/about-cancer/coping/family-friends/teens

IN-PERSON SUPPORT

Camp Kesem — Free week long summer camp offered to children and teens ages six to sixteen whose parents have passed away from cancer, are undergoing cancer treatment, or are cancer survivors. Visit campkesem.org to find camps offered in your state.

Kidskonnected.org- Monthly support group to talk with other teens whose parents have cancer. Visit their website to see locations where group meetings are being held.

BOOKS

Willhardt, Lynette. *Love Sick*. n.d. — "A collection of verse and image dedicated to those changed forever by cancer. It is a book for teens written by teens who share what their experience was like living with a parent who has cancer or coping with the death of a parent."

Vogel, Carole. *Will I Get Breast Cancer?* New York: Julian Messner, 1995. — A book addressing the specific needs of girls facing their mother's breast cancer.

Silver, Marc and Maya. *My Parent Has Cancer and It Really Sucks*. Illinois: Sourcebooks Fire, 2013. — "Author Maya Silver was fifteen when her mom was diagnosed with breast cancer in 2001. She and her dad, Marc, have combined their family's personal experience with advice from dozens of medical professionals and real stories from one hundred teens — all going through the same thing Maya did."

The National Cancer Institute. *When Your Parent Has Cancer: A Guide for Teens*. Maryland: National Cancer Institute, 2012. — Provided by The National Cancer Institute. Can be found for free by visiting http://www.cancer.gov/publications/patient-education/When-Your-Parent-Has-Cancer.pdf.

ONLINE RESOURCES THAT ARE NOT CANCER SPECIFIC

Loveisrespect.org — Online resource for teens that offers self care techniques, coping activities, journaling tips, and ways to get involved.

Yourlifeyourvoice.org — Online resource for teens that provides trained counselors to talk with over the phone, through email, or by text message.

Text 741-741 about "any type of crisis." Live trained counselors are available to you 24/7.

Cover Art Inspiration for Making It Mine

The cover art for Making It Mine was inspired by one beloved mother named Elisabeth, who like many of your parents, bravely fought cancer.

To make the cover, we scanned in parts of Elisabeth's favorite clothing and digitally collaged them together with new fabrics and hand-drawn illustrations.

Why was this process special?

The mixing of old and new expresses the way cancer changes our normal. Cancer takes what is familiar to us and throws some new, unfamiliar things into the mix. We find ourselves missing our old normal, wrestling with the overwhelming emotions of our present normal, and asking difficult questions about "new normals" all at once. Suddenly, anything familiar feels more special somehow, even something small like your parent's favorite clothes.

Wherever you are in this process, we stand with you.

Here's to you.

- Lauren Fueyo, cover artist

Acknowledgments

My parents, who have been the inspiration for this book
from its beginning.

My husband and best friend, Xander Bernhardt, who endlessly
edited and brainstormed. You have taught me how to love others
better, and this book is proof of that.

My graphic designer and brother-in-law, Samuel Bernhardt, who
brought this book to life in every way imaginable.

My illustrator, Nick Janouris, and photographer, Steven
McNamara, who allowed readers to meet our teens through their
pictures and portraits.

My cover art designer and friend, Lauren Fueyo, who has never
said no to any request that involves helping others.

Terri Trenchard, for your guidance throughout
the publishing process.

My mentor and oncology social worker, Jennifer Broaddus, who
has supported this book and the wellbeing of families facing cancer
more than any person I know.

Saint Agnes Cancer Institute, for making this book a reality in their
commitment to support each and every family who walks through
their doors.

And lastly, the teens and adults who fill the pages of this book
with their stories. My friends and my inspiration, you have given
something beautiful to the world.

Thank you, each of you.

Sources

American Cancer Society. 2014. "Family cancer syndromes."http://www.cancer.
org/cancer/cancercauses/geneticsandcancer/heredity-and-cancer

Awaken. http://www.awaken.com/2013/01/overcoming-f-e-a-r-false-evidence-
appearing-real/

Buechner, F. Accessed January 8. https://www.allgreatquotes.com/quotes/
family-28.shtml

Calendar Girls, directed by Nigel Cole, performance by Helen Mirren (1995;
Touchstone Pictures), DVD.

Chernoff, M. "10 things to remember when you feel unsure of yourself."
Accessed May 1. http://www.marcandangel.com/2015/11/18/10-
things-to-remember-when-you-feel-unsure-of-yourself/

Chernoff, M. "50 questions that will free your mind." Accessed May 1. http://
www.marcandangel.com/2009/07/13/50-questions-that-will-free-your-
mind/

Glen, C., L. Charles, (writers), and J. Burrows (director). Cheers. Season 11,
Episode 8. November 19, 1992.

Goodwin, G. Accessed July 1. https://www.pinterest.com/
pin/403494447837094736/

Huang, X., M. O'Connor, and S. Lee. 2014. "School-aged and adolescent
children's experience when a parent has non-terminal cancer: A
systematic review and meta-synthesis of qualitative studies." Psycho-
Oncology, 23(5), 493-506. doi: 10.1002/pon.3457.

Lindqvist, B., F. Schmitt, P. Santalahti, G. Romer, and J. Piha. 2007. "Factors associated with the mental health of adolescents when a parent has cancer." Scandinavian Journal of Psychology, 48(4), 345-351. doi: 10.1111/j.1467-9450.2007.00573.x.

Milne, A.A. 1926. Winnie-the-Pooh. Methuen & Co. Ltd. London.

Rhoades, J. Do More. Accessed July 1. https://www.scrapbook.com/poems/doc/15907.html

Roosevelt, E. 2011. You Learn by Living: Eleven Keys for a More Fulfilling Life. New York City, New York. Harper Perennial.

Shapiro, D., and E. Shapiro. 2013. "Overcoming F.E.A.R.: false evidence appearing real."

Silver, Marc and Maya. 2013. My Parent Has Cancer and It Really Sucks. Illinois: Sourcebooks Fire.

Wesley, J. 1799. Collection of Sermons.

Wilcox, E. 1898. Life's Scars. Frank Leslie's Popular Monthly.

Williams, M. 1922. The Velveteen Rabbit. New York. George H. Doran Company.

Willard, N. 1991. A Nancy Willard Reader. New York. Open Road Media.

You are wonderful. Accessed July 1. https://jemima.wordpress.com/2008/04/09/i-think-you-are-wonderful/

Made in the USA
Monee, IL
22 November 2019